*He was a man born
to shake the races of the earth,
a terror to all lands. . . .*

Priscus of Panium,
describing Attila the Hun

This book is dedicated to my horde of nieces and nephews.

Photographs © 2008: akg-Images, London: 70 top, 91 (Victor Adam/M.G. de Puy-Mirat, La France au Moyen-Age, Limoges), 68 top, 98 (Coll. Archiv f.Kunst & Geschichte), 70 bottom (Johann Ludwig Gottfried, Historische Chronica, Frankfurt/Coll. Archiv f.Kunst & Geschichte), 55, 69 bottom (Rainer Hackenberg), 45 (Alois Schreiber, Teutschland und die Teutschen, Karlsruhe, 1823/Coll. Archiv f.Kunst & Geschichte), 66 bottom (Westfalisches Schulmuseum), 54, 94 (W. Zimmerman, Geschichet des deutschen Volkes, Vol.1, Stuttgart, 1873/Coll. Archiv f.Kunst & Geschichte) 71 top, 111; Art Resource, NY: 106 (Adoc-photos), 84, 85 (Bildarchiv Preussischer Kulturbesitz), 79 (Vittore Carpaccio/Cameraphoto Arte, Venice), 25, 67 bottom (Francois Chauveau/HIP), 39, 57, 67 top left (Erich Lessing); Bridgeman Art Library International Ltd., London/New York: 87 (Church of Notre-Dame-de-Bonne-Nouvelle, Paris, France/Archives Charmet), 10 (Raymond Delamarre/ Private Collection/Archives Charmet), 59, 69 top (Museo Arqueologico Nacional, Madrid, Spain/ AISA); Corbis Images: 68 bottom, 105 (Bettmann), 77 (Michael Nicholson); Getty Images: 37, 66 top, 83 (Hulton Archive), 18, 19, 71 bottom, 75, 117 (Kean Collection); Hungarian National Gallery/Mór Than/FK 8209: 63, 69 center; Mary Evans Picture Library: 52, 68 center; The Granger Collection, New York: 43, 67 top right; The Image Works/Roger-Viollet: 29.

Illustrations by XNR Productions, Inc.: 4, 5, 8, 9
Cover art, page 8 inset by Mark Summers
Chapter art by Raphael Montoliu

Library of Congress Cataloging-in-Publication Data
Price, Sean.
Attila the Hun : leader of the barbarian hordes / Sean Stewart Price.
p. cm. — (A wicked history)
Includes bibliographical references and index.
ISBN-13: 978-0-531-21801-3 (lib. bdg.) 978-0-531-20737-6 (pbk.)
ISBN-10: 0-531-21801-5 (lib. bdg.) 0-531-20737-4 (pbk.)
1. Attila, d. 453 2. Huns. I. Title.
D141. P68 2009
936'.03092—dc22
[B]

2008040520

Tod Olson, Series Editor
Marie O'Neill, Art Director
Allicette Torres, Cover Design
SimonSays Design!, Book Design and Production

© 2009 Scholastic Inc.

Attila the Hun

Leader of the Barbarian Hordes

S E A N   S T E W A R T   P R I C E

Franklin Watts®
An Imprint of Scholastic Inc.
New York Toronto London Auckland Sydney
Mexico City New Delhi Hong Kong
Danbury, Connecticut

The World of Attila the Hun

Attila led the Huns against the mighty Roman Empire,
which had dominated Europe for centuries.

Atlantic
Ocean

Nor
Se

Rei
Catalaunian Field
Orléans •
Tro

GAUL

WEST
ROMAN
EMPIRE

NORTH AFRICA

miles
0   200   400

0   200   400
kilometers

KEY

A Attila is born around A.D. 400.

B In 408, led by King Uldin, the Huns cross
the Danube to launch their first invasion of
the Roman Empire.

C Attila is held hostage by the West Roman
Empire.

D After the death of his uncle in 435, Attila
becomes co-king of the Huns.

E In 447, Attila reaches the gates of
Constantinople, but fails to breach its walls.

F Attila is defeated by West Romans at the
Battle of Catalaunian Fields in 451.

G Attila withdraws from Italy after meeting
with Pope Leo I in 452.

H Attila dies in 453, on his wedding night.

* approximate locations

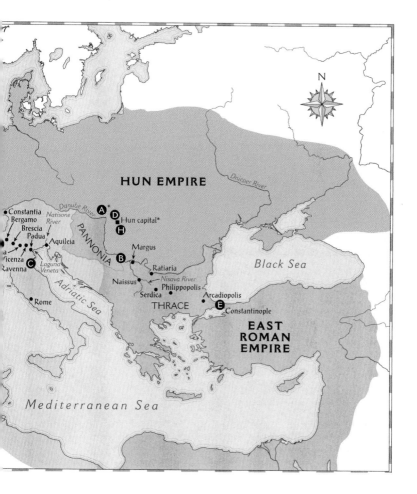

TABLE OF CONTENTS

A Wicked Web

A look at the allies and enemies of Attila the Hun.

Attila's Family and Allies

MUNDZUK
Attila's father, who died
when Attila was young

RUGA
Attila's uncle and chief Hun
king during Attila's youth

OCTAR
Attila's uncle and
co-ruler with Ruga

BLEDA
Attila's brother
and co-king

KREKA
Attila's senior wife,
the mother of his heir

ATTILA THE HUN

ILDICO
Attila's last wife, who was
with him when he died

ERNAK
Attila's most favored son

ELLAC
Attila's oldest son and heir

Barbarian Tribes

ALANS   BURGUNDIANS   FRANKS

GEPIDS   OSTROGOTHS   RUGIANS

SAXONS   SUEVES   SWABIANS

TAIFALI   THURINGIANS   VANDALS

VISIGOTHS

Attila's Enemies and Opponents

PRISCUS
East Roman civil
servant and writer

EMPEROR THEODOSIUS II
ruled the East Roman
Empire from 408 to 450

EMPEROR MARCIAN
leader of East Romans
after Theodosius's death

EMPEROR VALENTINIAN III
ruled the West Roman
Empire from 425 to 455

HONORIA
Valentinian's sister

FLAVIUS AETIUS
West Roman general
and leader (ally, then
enemy of Attila)

POPE LEO I
head of the Roman Catholic
Church from 440 to 461

THEODORIC
king of Visigoths
from 418 to 451

ATTILA THE HUN, c. A.D. 400–453

THE PEOPLE OF GAUL KNEW THE INVASION
was coming. Messengers from the east had brought the
news to this huge area in western Europe. But even to
those expecting it, the army of Attila the Hun must
have made a fearsome sight.

A quarter of a million men had made their way
up the Danube River from Pannonia, in present-day
Hungary. Most of them were bearded, rugged, and
stout. Swords swung from their waists. Some carried
bows and quivers of arrows slung across their backs.
The foot soldiers walked next to wagons loaded with
supplies. The cavalry rode horses with finely decorated
saddles and harnesses.

As Attila led his Hun army across the Rhine River
into present-day France, he saw the imposing works
of the greatest empire on earth. For 500 years, Gaul
had been a province of the Roman Empire, and the

Romans had left their mark there. Christian churches and cathedrals dominated many towns. A 100-foot-tall tower made of massive stone blocks guarded the city of Trier. A huge stone arch led the way into Reims.

Attila marched his men southwest, headed for a showdown with the mighty Roman army. When his men got hungry, they stopped to loot undefended towns for supplies. Most of the countryside was deserted, the Gauls having fled into the woods to escape the invading Huns. Those who chose to defend their homes often met a dreadful end. When the people of Metz refused to surrender to Attila, the Huns battered down the city's walls and slaughtered its inhabitants.

With a week's march to go before the two armies met, Attila arrived at the town of Troyes. His men entered and began to search the wood and thatch homes for food.

According to legend, a bishop named Lupus emerged from the cathedral to negotiate with Attila. Lupus introduced himself as a "man of God."

The Hun king supposedly replied, "I am Attila, the Scourge of God."

Lupus is said to have saved the town by offering himself to Attila as a hostage and guide. Attila left Troyes standing and moved on to battle the Roman army over the future of western Europe.

The encounter—or at least the story that emerged from it—gave Attila a name that stuck with him for centuries. The Hun king spent most of his life at war. His expert archers thundered through the countryside on horseback, spreading terror wherever they rode. His Christian victims saw the pagan Attila as a dark force of nature, like a disease or a terrible storm. They found only one explanation for the suffering he caused: Attila must have been a punishment sent by God.

PART 1

Rise of a Barbarian

CHAPTER 1

Prince of the Huns

Attila is taught the
WAYS OF HIS PEOPLE.

ATTILA WAS BORN AROUND THE YEAR 400. He belonged to a fierce group of nomads known as the Huns, who had battled their way from Asia into Europe a generation earlier.

The Huns were a loose collection of tribes, each tribe ruled by a different king. They raised sheep and cattle and moved often to find good pastureland. But they were best known for their horsemanship—and their bottomless hunger for loot. The Huns were expert thieves who swept into neighboring villages with little warning to steal gold, cloth, sugar, and any other luxuries they could find.

The Huns used surprise and speed to overwhelm their victims. A typical Hun warrior could shoot at least five arrows a minute from horseback. Hun horsemen galloped into villages, filled opposing fighters full of arrows, and then rode away without a scratch. In close fighting, the Huns used lassos to snare their enemies and drag them screaming to their deaths.

A Catholic monk named Jerome described a terrifying Hun raid that took place just before Attila was born: "They filled the whole earth with slaughter and panic as they flitted hither and thither on their swift horses. They were at hand everywhere before they were expected. By their speed, they outstripped rumor, and they took pity neither upon religion nor rank nor age nor wailing childhood."

After battle, a Hun king paid his warriors in loot to ensure their loyalty. The more booty a king provided, the more powerful he became.

Attila grew up in a family of powerful kings. His father, Mundzuk, ruled a tribe of Huns. Mundzuk died when Attila was young, perhaps in a bloody raid to gather loot for his followers.

Attila and his brother Bleda were probably raised by their uncles, King Octar and King Ruga. These two men rose through the ranks of kings to rule a great

VICTORIOUS HUNS with the heads of their victims on pikes. The Huns rarely bothered to occupy the lands they invaded. Instead, they stole wealth and slaves before moving on to their next target.

number of Hun warriors, and they expanded their power while Attila was growing up. They showed Attila what it took to gain and hold power among the Huns.

Like most Hun boys, Attila was very young when he began his training in the arts of war. He probably spent much of his childhood in the saddle. He'd ride for hours each day until he could stand in the stirrups or hang off the side of his horse while riding at top speed. He'd practice shooting arrows from his bow until his fingers were covered with deep calluses. Hun archers fired with accuracy from 100 yards or more. Attila would have learned to hit targets in all directions while riding at a full gallop.

In years past, when they roamed the plains of central Asia, Hun warriors used their skills to raid small villages and towns. By the time Attila came of age, a more formidable target was within reach. From their home on the Danube River, the Huns stood just on the border of the Roman Empire. The empire's mightiest cities, Constantinople and Rome, boasted the richest populations on earth. What a prize they would be for a young, ambitious warrior with a gift for leadership.

BARBARIANS INVADE ROME!

WHEN ATTILA WAS A BOY, THE ROMAN EMPIRE dominated the known world. But the ancient, massive empire was coming apart at the seams.

For eight centuries, Rome's legions of highly trained soldiers had conquered lands from Britain to the Middle East. At its peak, the empire covered nearly two million square miles. The Roman legions' military victories had brought great riches to Rome.

EAST AND WEST ROMAN EMPIRES

But for decades, the huge empire had been racked by civil wars, and by 395, the Romans had officially split their lands into western and eastern halves. The West Empire had its capital in Ravenna—although Rome remained its center of wealth and culture. The East Roman Empire was ruled from Constantinople (present-day Istanbul).

As the Huns pushed into Europe from Asia, they put even more strain on the crumbling Roman world. They also displaced tribes living on the outskirts of the East Roman Empire—the Ostrogoths, the

THE HUNS WERE JUST ONE of many tribes to invade Roman territory. Several tribes carved out their own kingdoms within the East and West Roman empires.

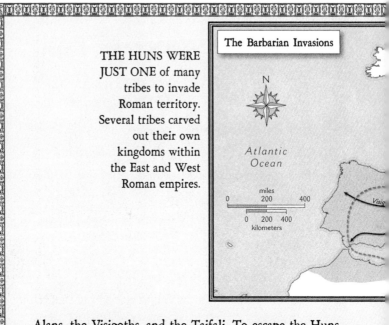

The Barbarian Invasions

N

Atlantic Ocean

miles
0   200   400

0   200   400
kilometers

Visi...

Alans, the Visigoths, and the Taifali. To escape the Huns, these tribes forced their way into Roman territory.

The Romans generally hated these refugees, whom they called "barbarians." The outsiders were said to be dirty, cruel, and uneducated. For these and other reasons, most Romans dismissed barbarians as inferior human beings. Romans generally thought barbarians were good enough to be slaves, soldiers, or even government officials. But they could never be the equal of a true Roman.

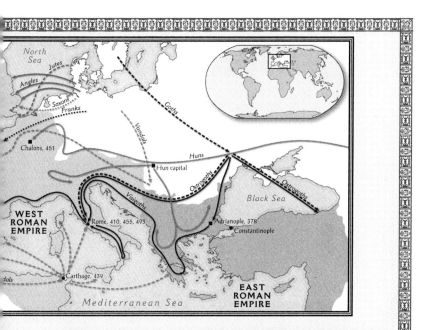

But the barbarians were there to stay. Many tribes set up their own homelands within the empire. The Roman army recruited tribesmen to fill its ranks. Eventually, most Roman generals came from barbarian roots.

To Attila and the Huns, the advance of the barbarian tribes signaled an opportunity. For centuries, the Romans had seemed untouchable. Was it possible that the Huns could bring them to their knees?

CHAPTER 2

Held Hostage

Barbarians challenge Rome's
supremacy, and young ATTILA
BECOMES A HOSTAGE IN ROME.

WHEN ATTILA WAS STILL A YOUNG BOY,
the Huns and other barbarian tribes began to challenge
the two parts of the Roman Empire—the East Roman
Empire and the West Roman Empire.

In 408, a Hun king named Uldin sent his men
thundering across the frozen Danube River into Thrace,
a province in the East Roman Empire. Hoping to avoid
a costly war, the Eastern Romans offered Uldin a bribe
to call off the attack.

BARBARIANS WERE AT THE GATES in 410, when
King Alaric led his Visigoths into Rome. Although the Visigoths
did little damage to the city, the invasion was humiliating
for the once-mighty Romans.

Uldin held out for a larger bribe, but he was betrayed by his own generals. They cut a separate deal with the Romans and withdrew across the Danube. Then the Romans wiped out what was left of Uldin's army.

Just two years later, in the West Roman Empire, a tribe of barbarians called the Visigoths fought their way into Rome itself. They decided to teach the city leaders a lesson and stripped the city of gold, statues, silks, and other valuables. It was the first time in almost 800 years that Rome had been sacked.

The West Roman Empire survived, but the defeat was a terrible shock to the Romans. In the East Roman Empire, Emperor Theodosius II's advisers agreed to send a pile of gold each year to the Huns to get them to stay on their side of the Danube.

West Romans were forced to negotiate with the Huns as well. They made one treaty that would change Attila's life: It called for Attila to be a hostage in the West Roman Empire. At the time, it was common for warring parties to guarantee a treaty by exchanging young men as hostages. These hostages were generally treated well. But if either side broke the treaty, the young men could lose their lives. With this risk hanging over him, Attila made the 500-mile journey to Ravenna, where he became a hostage in the court of Honorius, the emperor of the West Roman Empire.

The Romans enjoyed playing host to barbarian princes like Attila. In most cases, the young men became used to the Roman lifestyle, with its baths, silks, and fine wine. Sometimes they converted to Christianity. Most of them became thoroughly Romanized.

Attila, however, stubbornly remained a Hun. According to some accounts, he prowled around Honorius's palace like a caged animal. Supposedly, his hatred for the Romans grew. He began to study his enemies with the eye of a conqueror. He looked for weaknesses and found plenty.

Attila saw that both East and West were racked with constant conflict. Noble families started civil wars to determine who would be the next emperor.

The fighting used up valuable resources and placed greedy or incompetent leaders in control. The emperors imposed high taxes to pay for, among other things, armies that would keep them in power. The rulers and their families lived in luxury, while most Romans lived in poverty.

While the Romans fought among themselves, the Huns slowly gained strength.

To counter the barbarian threat, the leaders of the East Roman Empire ordered new naval patrols on the Danube River. In 413, they began building a massive new set of walls to protect Constantinople from invasion.

When Attila returned to the Hun kingdom, he found himself in a unique position. His uncles, Octar and Ruga, were no doubt gaining power as minor kings. Their power could only benefit Attila. And after years spent in the royal court in Ravenna, Attila knew better than any barbarian alive how to strike at the Romans' weak spots. It was only a matter of time before he used his knowledge to change the course of history.

A FELLOW HOSTAGE

IN 410, THE ROMANS SENT THEIR OWN HOSTAGE to the Huns. His name was Flavius Aetius. He was a teenager at the time, a little older than Attila. Most likely he lived well in the Hun capital and could come and go like an honored guest. He used his time with the Huns to become an excellent horseman and archer. He also learned to speak Hunnish and studied Hun culture.

More importantly, Aetius became friends with important Huns. One such friend was probably Attila's uncle, King Ruga. Another may have been Attila himself. We know nothing about their boyhood time together. But as men, Attila and Aetius would play a major role in each other's lives.

FLAVIUS AETIUS, who eventually became a great Roman general, learned from the Huns while he was their hostage.

PART 2

The Path to Power

A Force on the Danube

ATTILA'S UNCLES TAKE CHARGE of a growing empire.

IN 425, ATTILA WAS ABOUT 25 YEARS OLD. He had returned from the West Roman Empire and was no doubt enjoying his privileged status as a nephew of two powerful kings. Tribe by tribe, Ruga and Octar had brought more Huns under their control. Most likely, they bought the loyalty of thousands of warriors with raids into the East Roman Empire.

With Ruga and Octar in charge of a growing empire, Flavius Aetius, the former Roman hostage, returned to the Huns. He had a proposition for the two kings. Two years earlier, the Western emperor, Honorius, had died. Since then, the East and West Romans had been locked in a civil war to determine a successor. Aetius wanted the Huns to help him fight off the East Roman army. To make the deal attractive to the Hun kings, he had brought with him chests full of gold.

Octar and Ruga accepted the offer and sent an army galloping to Aetius's aid. Attila probably went with them. But by the time the Huns arrived in northern Italy, the struggle was over. The new Western emperor had been tortured and then executed at the order of the East Roman emperor, Theodosius II. Theodosius had then placed his cousin Valentinian III on the Western throne.

That did not stop the Huns. They stormed through Italy, looting as they rode.

Aetius, meanwhile, cut a deal with Emperor Theodosius. He paid Ruga and Octar to send their horsemen home. In return, Theodosius had Aetius named commander-in-chief of the West Roman army. As things settled down in Italy, Aetius went north to Gaul to battle barbarians on the border.

Ruga and Octar returned home with more wealth and power than before. With Aetius's approval, they took lands in Pannonia, a Roman province on the southwest bank of the Danube River. Backed by the Romans, Ruga and Octar gained more and more power over the lesser Hun kings.

In 432, Ruga and Octar tried to extend their empire even further. They took on a neighboring people called the Burgundians. But in the thick forests near the Rhine River, the Huns suffered an embarrassing defeat. They lost 10,000 men in battle—including their co-ruler Octar. Ruga now ruled the Huns alone.

Ruga proved to be a clever and ruthless king. In 433, he strengthened his alliance with the West Romans by helping Aetius win another civil war. He also launched raids against Theodosius in the East. By 434, he had harassed the East Romans into a deal that set a pattern for relations between the Huns and the East Roman Empire. In exchange for peace, Theodosius agreed to send the Hun king a payment of 350 pounds of gold each year.

Then, at the peak of his power, Ruga died. The only record of his death is a Christian account claiming that he was struck with a thunderbolt sent by God.

Attila probably went into mourning for his uncle. In keeping with Hun tradition, he cut off locks of his hair. He sliced his face with a knife, leaving ugly scars in his skin. Perhaps he knew that the scars would serve him well in the future. He'd do anything to strike fear into the hearts of his enemies—for along with his brother Bleda, Attila now ruled the Huns.

CHAPTER 4

On the Warpath

As co-king of the Huns, Attila
TAKES HIS ARMY INTO BATTLE.

HUGE CELEBRATIONS FOLLOWED THE mourning period after Ruga's death. Attila and his brother Bleda were crowned co-kings. Their subjects held singing, dancing, and riding competitions. Poets wrote flattering songs in praise of their new leaders' bravery and nobility.

At 35, Attila ruled a growing empire whose soldiers were feared throughout Europe. A Roman named Priscus, who later spent time at Attila's court, described the Huns as a warlike people, always alert and quick to reach for their weapons. They had broad shoulders, thick necks, and carried themselves proudly. "These men, in short, live in the form of humans but with the savagery of beasts," Priscus wrote.

ATTILA BECAME CO-KING of the Huns after he and his brother Bleda killed all possible rivals, even members of their own family.

To Romans like Priscus, all barbarians were savages. But during their first few years in power, Attila and Bleda probably lived up to the description. The brothers fought a fierce civil war to wipe out any Hun chiefs who challenged their hold on the throne. The few survivors fled for their lives.

Among the refugees were two of Attila's cousins, Mamas and Atakam. The cousins fled to Constantinople, where they probably assumed they were safe. But Attila was not about to leave his rivals in peace.

In 435, Attila and Bleda demanded a meeting with representatives of the East Roman emperor, Theodosius II. The Huns threatened to attack—unless they got more gold from Theodosius. They also demanded the return of their two cousins and any other Hun refugees living inside the empire.

Attila and Bleda mounted their horses and rode with a group of bodyguards to Margus, a border city on the Danube. There they met Theodosius's ambassadors. The Romans assumed they would be negotiating in royal fashion. They brought large tents and plenty of good food and wine.

Attila and Bleda refused to hold the meeting on Roman terms. In keeping with Hun tradition, they stayed in their saddles. The East Romans had no choice but to negotiate with the Huns on horseback.

The meeting signaled a shift in the balance of power along the Danube. With a newly unified army behind him, Attila and Bleda had made it clear to the Romans that they could not be ignored. The Roman ambassadors got the message. They agreed to double their gold payment, to 700 pounds per year. The Romans also agreed to hand over any Hun fugitives they could find.

Attila had a grim welcome waiting for his two cousins. The Hun king had Mamas and Atakam

ATTILA AND HIS MEN REFUSED TO DISMOUNT
during a meeting with the Romans. Attila (middle)
saw no reason to respect Roman traditions.

impaled on sharpened wood poles. His guards stuck the poles upright in the ground, where the prisoners spent hours in agony before they died.

Attila and Bleda then turned their attention to their old friend Aetius. For more than a decade, Aetius had been battling the Burgundians, who had been carving out their own kingdom in a rich area in southeastern Gaul.

Around 437, with help from Attila, Aetius launched an attack on the upstart nation. He killed thousands of Burgundians and drove the rest into a quiet existence in the rocky mountains called the Alps.

There would be no peace and quiet for the king of the Huns, however. Just a few years after the campaign against the Burgundians, Attila's truce with the East Roman Empire began to break down. Emperor Theodosius fell behind on the payments his ambassadors had agreed to in Margus. Attila could not let the slight go unpunished. To keep his people happy and loyal, he needed a constant supply of loot.

One winter's day around 440, Roman merchants were gathered at a trade fair in Constantia, an East Roman fortress near the Danube River. Hun fighters disguised as traders were scattered throughout the crowd. Suddenly, the Huns turned on the East Romans, stabbing the unsuspecting merchants and slitting their throats. Roman soldiers, caught off guard, were also butchered.

Theodosius protested, but the Huns insisted that they had been provoked. According to Attila, a Christian bishop from Margus had been sneaking across the Danube to rob the graves of Hun kings. Attila demanded that the thief be turned over to the Huns.

The bishop decided to save his own skin. He made a deal with the Huns and secretly arranged for the gates of Margus to be thrown open. Bloodthirsty attackers poured in. Their rampage was so complete that the town was never rebuilt.

After the sack of Margus, Attila decided to press his advantage. Emperor Theodosius had sent thousands of troops to help the West Romans in North Africa, where the Vandals had invaded. With these East Roman troops out of the way, the Huns had a clear path 500 miles down the Danube River, all the way to Constantinople.

In 441, Attila led his army southeast along the Danube. They seized at least two more cities. But by this time, Theodosius had called his army back from North Africa. He ordered that new coins be made to pay for the war against the Huns.

Attila's assault stalled. Perhaps he decided that an attack on Constantinople would prove too costly. Perhaps he negotiated a share of Theodosius's new coins for himself. Whatever his reason, Attila retreated to his side of the river and waited to fight another day.

WHO WERE THE VANDALS?

THE HUNS STRUCK FEAR INTO THE HEARTS OF the Romans. But their fellow barbarians, the Vandals, did so much damage to the empire that their name came to mean "senseless destruction."

The Vandals originally lived in what is now Germany. They were neighbors of the Visigoths and the Ostrogoths. Around the year 406, the Huns pushed them west into Gaul. The Vandals terrorized local tribes there before moving south into Iberia (modern-day Spain).

The Vandals then crossed the Straits of Gibraltar into North Africa in 429. During the next decade, they swept through the richest province in the West Roman Empire.

The invasion created such a disaster for the Romans that East and West banded together in an effort to fight off the Vandals. The last Vandals were finally killed or enslaved by the East Romans in 534.

VANDALS MARCH toward Rome.

43

CHAPTER 5

Sword of the War God

Attila becomes SOLE KING OF THE HUNS.

FRESH FROM HIS CAMPAIGN AGAINST THE East Roman Empire, Attila returned home to consolidate power. He did so at the expense of his own family.

In 444, Attila murdered Bleda, his brother and fellow ruler.

The coup probably took place without a bloody civil war. Attila would have left the bodies of Bleda's family

ATTILA TAKES "THE SWORD OF GOD" from a herdsman.
According to the legends of his people, Attila now had the
power to win every battle and conquer the whole world.

and supporters hanging where they had been impaled as a warning to any potential opponents. Yet Attila did show some mercy. Bleda had several wives, and the most important one was allowed to live.

Attila now stood alone as king of the Huns. Around this time, a legend emerged to convince his subjects that their leader had no equal. The story passed by word of mouth from village to village. It was said that a herdsman had been out in his fields and had seen a cow limping on a bloody foot. He followed the trail of blood and found a sword sticking out of the ground.

The herdsman took the sword to Attila. The king took one look at it and announced that the lowly herdsman had found a long-lost treasure—the sword of the Hun war god. Whoever carried it had the power to win any war, defeat any foe. Attila rejoiced that it had been given to him. Then he made sure that the story spread quickly among the Huns.

Many rulers of the time claimed to be favored by the gods. But Attila acted like a man who truly had divine support. According to Priscus, the Roman historian, Attila "was haughty in the way he carried himself. [He cast] his eyes about him on all sides so that the proud man's power was to be seen in the very movements of his body."

Attila naturally liked to hear people praise him. At least two court poets wrote songs celebrating his courage and leadership. The poets sang their songs at festivals and other important events.

When he claimed sole control of the Huns, Attila was in his mid-forties, old for a man of his time. But it was hard to imagine him suffering a major defeat. His terrifying power was just reaching its peak. And Attila was already scheming to bring the East Romans to their knees.

ATTILA'S SPIRITUAL WORLD

THE HUNS CLUNG FIERCELY TO THEIR OWN gods, even after many barbarian tribes followed the Romans' lead and adopted Christianity.

Not much is known about the Hun religion. But the Hun gods were most likely inspired by the wind, rain, lightning, and other forces of nature.

Archeologists have found some evidence of the Huns' religious practices. The Huns cut off horses' heads and placed them on poles around their camps. Most likely, they thought the heads kept evil spirits away.

Attila himself was deeply spiritual. He hung on the words of fortunetellers and seers. In fact, because of one mystical prediction, he favored his youngest son, Ernak, while largely ignoring the rest of his family. Apparently, Attila had been told that when he died the Huns would suffer a great defeat. Only Ernak, the fortuneteller said, could bring them back to greatness.

HUNS OFFERED their gods sacrifices before battle.

C H A P T E R   6

Blood in the Balkans

Attila's men cut A DEADLY PATH TO CONSTANTINOPLE.

EARLY ON THE MORNING OF JANUARY 26, 447, a massive earthquake rocked Constantinople. Tremors shook the ground for just a few seconds. But the shock was enough to cause roofs to collapse and foundations to crack. In the dust-filled sunrise, the horrified East Romans saw that the quake had torn gaping holes in their city's walls. Constantinople lay wide open to invasion.

The nightmare was just beginning. Four solid days of rain followed the earthquake. Water poured through the streets and collapsed already tottering buildings. Many people were trapped in the ruins and drowned. Dirty drinking water caused an outbreak of disease. The smell of death from decaying bodies filled the air.

To many East Romans, the disaster seemed like divine punishment for their sins. To Attila, it must have seemed as though the war god was smiling on him. Tensions had been mounting between the Huns and the East Romans. Once again, Theodosius had missed his annual payments. Attila longed for war, and the quake-ravaged Eastern capital now seemed vulnerable to attack.

Just after the earthquake, Attila sent his mighty army south and east, into the East Roman province of Thrace. As they swept down along the Danube River, the Huns displayed an effective new skill. Unlike other barbarian leaders, Attila had learned the art of siege warfare from the Romans. He could now seize fortified cities.

City by city, the Huns advanced toward Constantinople. They captured Ratiara and Naissus near the Danube. Then they pushed south down the Nisava River, overrunning Serdica, Philippopolis, and Arcadiopolis. Each time the Huns besieged a city, they surrounded its walls with giant towers made of wood. Archers stood on platforms at the top of each tower, protected by screens of wood and animal hide. From their lofty perches, the archers rained arrows over the city walls. Meanwhile, Attila's men on the ground hauled battering rams with iron points to the city gates. They pounded away at the gates until holes opened up and the Huns could begin to pour through.

Small villages made an easier prize for the Huns, whose reputation for brutality spread as they advanced. In each village, people saw a cloud of dust as the Huns approached. Soon, they heard the thunder of thousands of hooves. By then, escape was impossible. The Hun horsemen swept in and rounded up everyone they could find. Those who resisted were slaughtered.

ATTILA LEARNED FROM THE ROMANS how to attack
walled cities. His men used huge battering rams tipped with iron
to smash through gates and other weak points.

Villagers who surrendered to the Huns had a chance to survive. But their lives would never be the same. The Huns separated men from women. They made slaves of the young women, with higher-ranking Huns getting first choice. Attila's generals gave young male captives two terrible options: Join the Hun army or be killed on the spot.

The Huns generally freed the very old and the very young—but only after robbing or burning their homes. All villagers had to treat their conquerors with reverence. One disrespectful comment could provoke a rampage of killing. The Huns were notorious for the cruel tortures they inflicted on their captives. And Attila's horsemen were known to run down victims just for the thrill of the chase.

Twenty years after the invasion, a monk named Callinicus clearly recalled Attila's deadly march. "There was so much killing and bloodletting that no one could number the dead. They pillaged the churches and monasteries, and slew the monks and

HUN HORSEMEN SLAUGHTER foot soldiers from
another barbarian tribe as they cut across Europe.

[nuns]. . . . They so devastated Thrace that it will
never rise again and be as it was before."

Leaving a path of devastation behind them, the
Huns finally closed in on the biggest prize of all:
Constantinople.

JEWEL OF THE EAST

BY 447, CONSTANTINOPLE HAD SERVED AS HOME to East Roman emperors for a century. In that time, they had built a city like the world had never seen.

At the heart of the capital, the emperor's palace covered millions of square feet. Its mosaic floors were the largest on earth. Near the palace, a giant stadium called the Hippodrome regularly hosted 100,000 spectators, who came out to root for their favorite teams in chariot races.

By the time Attila reached its gates, Constantinople was considered invincible. It occupied a peninsula protected on three sides by water. On land stood a fearsome line of defenses. Any attacking army first had to cross a moat 65 feet wide and 30 feet deep. If attackers made it past the moat, they faced an outer wall 30 feet high and an inner wall twice as high. Breaching the walls was a near-impossible task, even for Attila's fearsome war machine.

THEODOSIUS II had these walls built to protect Constantinople from the Huns.

CHAPTER 7

Saving Constantinople

With Attila closing in, the East Romans SCRAMBLE TO REBUILD THEIR WALLS.

For months, the residents of Constantinople heard rumors of Attila's approach. With the walls crumbling from the earthquake, panic spread through the city. Emperor Theodosius, a Christian, looked to his God for help. He led 10,000 people barefoot through the quake-damaged streets to demonstrate their religious devotion. Each person on

THEODOSIUS II RULED from Constantinople, the mightiest city in the world. But when an earthquake destroyed the city's walls, the East Romans seemed at the mercy of the Huns.

the solemn march prayed for safety from the Huns.

The answer to their prayers came from an unusual source—the city's sports fans. People in Constantinople followed chariot racing the way people today follow baseball or football. Chariot fans backed one of four main teams: the Blues, Greens, Reds, or Whites.

Constantinople's leaders used the racing rivalries to their advantage. They organized each team's followers into work gangs and assigned them sections of the city's damaged defenses. The competitors rebuilt Constantinople's walls in two months.

As Attila neared the Eastern capital, he encountered a force of Theodosius's soldiers and quickly defeated them. But when he arrived outside the city, he found it sealed up tight. Even Attila's siege engines were no match for the repaired walls of Constantinople.

Denied the prize of the East Roman Empire, Attila ravaged the countryside. Before long, however, disease began to thin the ranks of Attila's army. Dysentery, which causes severe diarrhea, killed thousands of his men. "He who was skilled in shooting with the bow, sickness of the bowels overthrew him," one Roman writer gloated. "The riders of the steed slumbered and slept, and the cruel army was silenced."

Both sides realized that they had reached a stalemate. Attila could not get his hands on Theodosius, and Theodosius could not drive off Attila.

The two rulers agreed to a peace. But the terms fell heavily in Attila's favor. Theodosius agreed once more to hand over any Huns who had taken refuge in the East. Some refugees asked their Roman comrades to kill them—rather than be turned over to Attila. Theodosius also agreed to triple Attila's annual payments. The East

Romans now had to come up with 2,100 pounds of gold each year. It was a huge sum, and quite a few wealthy Romans would have to sell their jewelry and family valuables to help meet Attila's price.

Attila also demanded—and received—a piece of East Roman territory. The Romans agreed to evacuate the rest of the Roman province of Pannonia. This zone would separate the Hun homeland from the East Roman Empire.

Strangers rarely penetrated Attila's homeland on the Danube River. But one expedition was about to make its

way to the Hun king's doorstep, with a secret and deadly mission.

EMPEROR THEODOSIUS PAID ATTILA 2,100 pounds of gold each year to make sure the Huns stayed on their side of the Danube River.

CHAPTER 8

In Attila's Court

Outsiders visit the Hun homeland
WITH MYSTERIOUS INTENT.

In 449, A GROUP OF DIPLOMATS SET OUT from Constantinople, bound for the Hun capital. The group included a few Hun envoys returning from a meeting with Theodosius. Joining them were several East Romans with orders to speak with Attila. Among the Romans was the writer Priscus. His record of the trip would become the only eyewitness account of the Hun leader's life and habits.

The journey to the Hun capital gave the East Romans a chilling look at Attila's military achievements. The trip took them through Thrace, which the Hun army had overrun two years before. Signs of the devastation were everywhere. In the city of Naissus, for instance, bones from the slaughter still littered the riverbank.

Unknown to Priscus, two of his traveling companions harbored secret plans to avenge the destruction of Thrace. Theodosius's chief adviser had bribed a tribal ruler named Ediko, an ally of the Huns, to assassinate Attila. Ediko had agreed to conspire with an East Roman translator named Vigilas.

The small group of diplomats arrived at Attila's home in the summer of 449. The Hun capital seemed like a tiny village next to Constantinople. To Priscus, it looked like a collection of huts strung together by a few dirt roads. Attila's home naturally stood out from the rest. It was made of wood and surrounded by a tall wooden fence. All the boards had been highly polished.

Attila returned from a trip just as the diplomats arrived, and Priscus witnessed his reception. Rows of beautiful young women marched in front of Attila as he rode into town. They waved white linen banners above their heads and sang songs praising their king.

The Romans began their meetings with Attila, and Priscus noticed immediately that most of the king's close advisers came from outside the Hun tribe. These foreign advisers knew the outside world. They spoke and wrote both Latin and Greek, the languages of the Romans. Their skills helped Attila understand and communicate with his enemies. But Attila may have had another reason to surround himself with foreigners. He had killed many Huns in his rise to power. With so many enemies among his own people, it might have been hard to find advisers he could trust.

Following Hun tradition, Attila had a large number of wives. Priscus visited the home of his chief wife, Kreka. She and Attila had three sons. The oldest, Ellac, was the king's heir. Like a good diplomat, Priscus brought valuable presents to Kreka. Her house, he reported, was beautifully decorated. "[I] came upon her lying on a soft spread," he wrote. "The floor was covered with mats of

THE COURT OF KING ATTILA. Priscus, the East Roman writer (bottom right), noted that Attila surrounded himself with foreign advisers—perhaps because he had made enemies of so many of his fellow Huns.

felted wool. A number of servants were waiting on her in a circle, and the maidservants, sitting on the floor in front of her, were embroidering fine linens to be placed as ornament over their barbarian clothes."

Attila's own house was even more luxurious. His bedroom was so large that it doubled as a banquet hall. But for a man who considered himself a mighty conqueror, his personal habits remained modest. At a dinner Priscus attended, the guests ate from silver plates while Attila preferred a simple wood platter. "He showed himself temperate in all other ways too," Priscus noted. "His dress was plain, having care for nothing other than to be clean. Nor was the sword by his side, nor the clasps of his barbarian boots, nor the bridle of his horse, like those of other [Huns], adorned with gold or gems or anything of high price."

As the Huns celebrated Attila's return, the Romans' assassination plot quickly unraveled. Ediko decided he could not go through with the plan. He told Attila everything, leaving himself to the Hun king's mercy.

Attila could have had everyone—including the innocent Priscus—put to death. Instead, he played dumb for six weeks. He waited until he had enough proof of the translator Vigilas's guilt. Then he detained only Vigilas and let the others go.

Rather than kill the would-be assassin, Attila decided to embarrass Theodosius. He held Vigilas as a hostage and sent two Huns back to Constantinople to deliver a message.

The Hun messengers appeared before the emperor, and one of the Huns spoke Attila's words. Theodosius, according to the Hun king, was like "a miserable house slave" trying to kill his master. "Who now," Attila wanted to know, "is the barbarian and who the more civilized?"

Attila demanded another large payment from Theodosius, who gave in yet again. Satisfied for now, Attila showed no desire to seek revenge against his old rival. But it would not be long before the Hun war machine had a new target.

Attila the Hun in Pictures

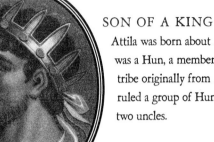

SON OF A KING

Attila was born about A.D. 400. He was a Hun, a member of a fierce tribe originally from Asia. His father ruled a group of Huns, as did his two uncles.

THE HORRIBLE HUNS

The Huns were best known for their horsemanship—and their hunger for loot. "They took pity neither upon religion nor rank nor age," one observer noted.

THE ROMAN LEGIONS

These highly trained soldiers had enabled the Romans to dominate the known world for 800 years.

ROMANS VS. BARBARIANS

Romans considered outsiders uncivilized and called them barbarians. Here, a Roman soldier is about to stab a barbarian.

ROME SACKED!

When Attila was still a boy, barbarian tribes started to challenge the Romans' supremacy. In 410, a tribe called the Visigoths invaded and sacked Rome.

KING OF THE HUNS

In 444, Attila gained sole power among the Huns after killing off all possible rivals, including his own brother.

INVADING THE EAST

In 447, Attila invaded the East Roman Empire, headed for the capital city of Constantinople. Along the way, he borrowed a trick from the Romans—he used battering rams to break down the walls of cities.

UNDER SEIGE

Attila had also learned from the Romans to use catapults to hurl large stones at city walls.

SHAKEDOWN

For years, Attila had been blackmailing Theodosius II, emperor of the East Roman Empire: Pay in gold coins or be invaded by the Huns.

BUNGLED PLOT

East Roman diplomats came to Attila's house in the summer of 449 with a secret plot to kill him. However, Attila learned of the plot and later humiliated Theodosius, saying the emperor was like "a miserable house slave" trying to kill his master.

PRIZE OF THE EAST ROMAN EMPIRE

Attila failed to take Constantinople, the wealthiest city in the world.

ATTILA TURNS WEST

Stymied in the East Roman Empire, Attila turned his attention to the Western Empire. In 451, he invaded Gaul, which was divided between the warring Visigoths and Romans.

FINAL GLORY

Catalaunian Fields was the site of the last great battle of West Roman history. Allied with the Visigoths, the Romans defeated Attila's army of 250,000 barbarians.

BARBARIANS AT THE GATES

In 452, Attila invaded present-day Italy and neared Rome itself. According to legend, Pope Leo I convinced Attila to withdraw.

FITTING END

During his wedding night in 453, Attila choked on his own blood and died. The unexpected death doomed the Huns, who were soon pushed out of Europe by the East Roman army and rival barbarian tribes.

PART 3

Attila Turns West

CHAPTER 9

Honoria's Honor

Attila gets a strange plea for help—
and uses it as AN EXCUSE TO
MAKE WAR.

IN 450, ATTILA'S ENEMY, EMPEROR Theodosius II, died. But in the Hun capital, the news hardly called for celebration. For years, Attila had been able to extort higher and higher payments from Theodosius. The new emperor, Marcian, would not be such a pushover. He abruptly cut off the flow of gold to the Huns. When Attila sent envoys to threaten him, the emperor replied that he reserved gold for his friends. To his enemies, he gave the iron in his sword.

Marcian's hard line forced Attila into a tough choice: Try again to sack Constantinople, or find another supply of loot.

Rather than batter his army against the massive walls of the Eastern capital, Attila looked to the West.

In the past decade, the Huns' old Roman friend

MARCIAN ENRAGED Attila by refusing to pay the bribes Theodosius had agreed to. Unlike Theodosius, Marcian had served as a soldier in wars against the barbarians.

Aetius had worked hard to keep the West Roman Empire from falling apart. But by 450, the Romans had become just one more tribe jockeying for power with their neighbors. In North Africa, the Vandals had taken over Rome's wealthiest province. In Europe, the Visigoths, the Alans, the Sueves, and other peoples had seized huge chunks of Roman land.

The West Roman Empire had never been weaker. Attila recognized the opportunity and set his sights on

Gaul. Since 425, Aetius had been trying to maintain Roman control over the region. But it was no easy task. A tribe in the northeast, the Franks, stubbornly guarded their independence. In the southwest, the Visigoths had their own kingdom. With bands of thieves running wild in between, Gaul was ripe for invasion. All Attila needed was an excuse to attack.

In 450 the excuse arrived in the form of a letter from the sister of Valentinian III, the West Roman emperor. Her name was Honoria, and she wanted Attila's help.

Honoria had been discovered plotting against her brother with a lover. Most likely, she had planned to marry the man, murder her brother, and seize the throne. But Valentinian's advisers discovered the plot and had her lover executed. Then they forced Honoria into an engagement with a man she despised.

Enraged, Honoria sent her message to Attila. With it she included money and a gold ring. It's not clear what Honoria intended, but Attila decided to interpret her gesture as a marriage proposal. He sent off a message to Valentinian, demanding that he, Attila, be allowed to marry Honoria. The two of them, he added, must be given control over half the empire.

Valentinian most likely thought that Attila had gone mad. He informed the Hun king that Honoria was engaged to someone else and that women had no right to power. Attila supposedly sent an ambassador back to Ravenna with a simple message: "[Attila] has ordered you, through me, to prepare your palace for him."

VALENTINIAN III was a weak ruler who had lost territory to the Vandals, Visigoths, and many other tribes. In 450, his own sister plotted to have him killed.

CHAPTER 10

Invasion of Gaul

ATTILA STRIKES TERROR
in western Europe.

IN EARLY 451, ATTILA'S WAR MACHINE began to rumble toward Gaul and the kingdom of the Visigoths. At least 250,000 men marched across what is now Germany. They moved northwest along the Danube to the Rhine River, which had served as the border between the Hun kingdom and Gaul. The Huns carried little food or water. They lived off the land, looting towns and villages as they went.

ATTILA INVADED GAUL in 451. Legend has it that during
this campaign, a Christian leader named Ursula enraged Attila by
refusing his demand that she marry him. Here she kneels in
prayer as her followers are slaughtered by the Huns.

The massive army moved slowly. Wagons and horses had to be ferried across rivers swollen by spring rains. At each crossing, Attila's troops stopped to cut logs and build rafts. The Huns managed only about 13 miles a day. Their slow pace gave most villagers time to escape with whatever valuables they could carry.

Attila wanted to reach the heart of Gaul before Aetius could organize resistance. To keep his army moving, Attila simply bypassed most fortified cities. The Huns did manage to capture the city of Metz after a short fight. According to Roman reports, the inhabitants were slaughtered. Many died in the flames that destroyed the city.

The Huns continued their march through Gaul, leaving a trail of violence that has given rise to countless folktales about Attila's cruelty. In the city of Reims, most people fled before the Huns arrived. The local bishop, Nicasius, supposedly stayed and held a special church service. He was singing a hymn when a Hun soldier cut off his head. According to legend, the bishop's head continued to sing even after it was severed from his body. The Roman Catholic Church later declared Nicasius a saint.

Another story involves a devoutly religious woman named Ursula, who had a large following of Christian worshippers. She was said to be a great beauty who had refused to marry in order to devote herself to God. Attila himself supposedly saw Ursula and asked that she become his wife. She refused. So he killed Ursula and thousands of women who were her followers. Like Nicasius, she was declared a saint by the Catholic Church.

Attila moved on to Troyes, where he acquired the nickname "Scourge of God" during his encounter with the bishop, Lupus.

The Scourge of God, however, was about to suffer his own punishment at the hands of an old ally.

CHAPTER 11

The Rescue of Orléans

The Roman cavalry STOPS ATTILA IN THE NICK OF TIME.

ATTILA INVADED GAUL EXPECTING THE resistance to be divided and weak. The two strongest powers in the region, the Romans and Visigoths, had fought over control of Gaul for decades. Tensions between the two enemies were always high.

Aetius, however, had realized that he needed help from the Visigoths; his army was too small to survive against Attila's massive force. So he

ATTILA THE HUN, SCOURGE OF GOD, left a trail of
death as he marched through Gaul. Aetius, the great
Roman general who had once lived with the Huns,
claimed that Attila was the "enemy of all nature."

swallowed his pride and sent ambassadors to form an alliance with Theodoric, king of the Visigoths. Aetius's ambassadors told Theodoric that Attila was the "enemy of all nature." The Hun king not only threatened both the Romans and the Visigoths, he wanted to "enslave the whole world." To stop him, the Romans and the Visigoths had to bury their disagreements and join forces against the Huns.

Theodoric supposedly announced his reply in front of his generals. "Romans," he said, "you shall have what you desire. You have made Attila our foe as well."

Aetius led his Roman army to meet the Visigoths, and the combined force raced north to stop Attila.

The Huns, meanwhile, arrived at the gates of Orléans, one of the biggest cities in Gaul. Attila's men

A MEDIEVAL WOODPRINT of the Huns' invasion of Gaul. Attila had attacked with some 250,000 bloodthirsty warriors, a fearsome force that would be remembered for centuries.

surrounded the city. They hammered at the city walls with battering rams and catapults.

The Romans of Orléans were terrified. The deadly *thud, thud, thud* of the Hun battering rams echoed throughout the city. Panic-stricken people flung themselves to the ground in prayer.

Attila ignored an offer of surrender from the city's leaders and sent his men storming through the shattered walls. The looting began almost immediately. Yet even as the Huns poured in, a watchman yelled to everyone who could hear: The Roman cavalry were approaching in the distance! "It is the aid of God!" cried the city's bishop.

Attila quickly realized that his enemies had united against him. With a combined force of Romans and Visigoths bearing down on him, he could not defend the city whose walls he had just smashed. Nor were the woods around Orléans a good place to deploy his men. He needed a flat area where his archers could maneuver on horseback.

The Hun king pulled his men out of Orléans before the Romans could cut off his escape. But with Aetius in pursuit, a major battle would be hard to avoid.

ACCORDING TO SOME ACCOUNTS, a Christian named Genevieve prayed for the city of Paris to be protected from Attila. The Hun king bypassed Paris and laid siege to Orléans.

Attila consulted his fortunetellers and priests. They read the future by examining the blood and guts of a slaughtered cow. The fortunetellers hesitated and then told their king what they had seen: Fighting a battle now would mean a terrible defeat for the Huns, but an enemy commander would die in the battle.

To Attila, it seemed like a risk worth taking. Aetius, he reasoned, must be the doomed commander. Without Aetius's skilled leadership, the West Roman Empire would crumble. It would be worth a defeat on the battlefield to get the great Roman commander out of the way. The Huns would retreat—and then return in force to bring the weakened empire to its knees.

The king of the Huns decided to fight. He chose a battlefield near the town of Châlons called the Catalaunian Fields. It was a wide-open plain dominated by a small hill. All of it would soon be drenched in blood.

CHAPTER 1 2

A Battle for the Ages

ATTILA PAYS A HIGH PRICE at the Catalaunian Fields.

IN THE MIDDLE OF JUNE 451, ON AN OPEN plain in the center of Gaul, close to half a million men squared off for control of ancient Europe. On one side stood Aetius's force——Romans, Visigoths, and Alans dressed in armor made of leather or bronze scales. Thousands more sat astride armored horses, ready to charge on a signal from their captain. Across the plain, Attila's men gathered on the banks of the Marne

River. Gepids, Ostrogoths, Rugians, Swabians, and Thuringians filled the ranks of Attila's infantry. Deadly Hun archers rode horseback, each with a quiver of 60 arrows at the ready.

Despite the diversity in Attila's army, there was no doubt who was in charge. "The leaders of the various nations hung upon Attila's nod like slaves," wrote a Visigoth historian named Jordanes, "and when he gave a sign, even by a glance, without a murmur each stood forth in fear and trembling."

As the battle began, the two sides raced to control the hill rising from the plain. The Visigoths arrived first and took control of the summit. They swept down on the Huns, driving them back into their own lines.

Attila regrouped and prepared to lead his men headlong into the center of the enemy. According to Jordanes, the Hun king rallied his soldiers with a speech. "Now show your cunning, Huns, now show your deeds of arms," he said. "Let the wounded exact in return the death of his foe. Let the unwounded revel in slaughter

ATTILA DIRECTS HIS MEN at the Battle of
Catalaunian Fields. The Visigoths, Alans, and Romans had
allied to oppose the Hun army.

of the enemy. . . . Why should fortune have made the Huns victorious over so many nations unless it were to prepare them for the joy of this conflict?"

With the clank of swords and the thunder of footsteps, the Huns unleashed a ferocious attack. A force of Ostrogoths stormed the hill. Foot soldiers advanced across the plain. The Hun cavalry led the charge, darting toward Aetius's main force. Mounted Hun archers raced in, launched a volley of arrows, and then retreated to let the next wave take their place. The sky filled with the deadly whistle of arrows. Most of them hit shields or armor or missed altogether. But the clouds of missiles found plenty of targets. Romans and Visigoths crumpled to the ground, wounded or dead.

The Romans and the Visigoths pressed forward through the hail of arrows. They fought their way into the lines of Hun foot soldiers, and the clang of iron swords rang out above the battle. The fighting grew "fierce, confused, monstrous, unrelenting," according to Jordanes.

Slowly the Romans and Visigoths pushed the Hun army back. Attila and his bodyguards retreated to a circle of wagons in the rear of the Hun lines. Arrows from the Roman archers began to fall around them.

Aetius knew that he had the Huns confused and nearly surrounded. Perhaps one more push would wipe out the dreaded Attila.

But the Visigoths suddenly turned away from the fighting. King Theodoric was missing. They searched the battlefield frantically for some time, easing the pressure on the Huns.

Finally, the Visigoths uncovered their leader's body amidst a pile of corpses. "They found him where the dead lay thickest, as happens with brave men," wrote Jordanes. "They honored him with songs and bore him away in the sight of the enemy. You might have seen the bands of [Visigoths] shouting with dissonant cries and paying the honors of death while the battle still raged."

THEODORIC'S BODY is carried off the battlefield at Catalaunian
Fields. The death of their king may have demoralized the Visigoths.

The Roman attack continued even while the
Visigoths mourned their king. Shaken by the onslaught,
Attila panicked. He ordered his men to build a funeral
pyre for him. Attila knew what happened to barbarian
leaders who fell into Roman hands. In 52 B.C., Julius
Caesar had captured a barbarian king in Gaul. Caesar
paraded his captive though the streets of Rome in chains
and later had him strangled.

Attila would rather go up in flames than suffer that
fate. But his aides convinced him that the battle was not
yet lost. The Huns might still salvage a small victory
from this terrible defeat.

Chapter 13

Fight Another Day

Aetius gives Attila AN UNEXPECTED REPRIEVE.

AROUND 9 P.M. THE SUN FINALLY SET ON the Catalaunian Fields. The gathering dark made it impossible to tell friend from foe. The clatter of swords and the bellowing of men in combat died away. Groans and screams from the wounded filled the survivors' ears. Dying men called out for their mothers or wives. Injured horses whinnied in pain.

Sweating, exhausted men stumbled back to their own side of the battlefield and tried to find something to eat or drink. A small stream ran through the battlefield, colored red with blood. Jordanes writes that "those whose wounds drove them to slake their parching thirst drank water mingled with gore."

Attila gathered his surviving soldiers behind the circle of wagons, the river at their backs. The Romans had cornered the Hun king, but they had not defeated him. In fact, according to Jordanes, Attila terrified the Romans even in his weakened state. "He was like a lion pierced by hunting spears, who paces to and fro before the mouth of his den and dares not spring, but ceases not to terrify the neighborhood by his roaring."

Attila wondered what the morning would bring. Would Aetius launch an all-out assault on the Huns? Or would he wait and wear Attila's army down with a siege? Either way, Attila couldn't hold out for long.

As it turned out, Aetius was planning to wait until his Romans had starved out the Hun camp. But the Visigoths had other ideas. Distracted by the loss of their king, they decided to desert the battlefield. It may be that Theodoric's death set off a power struggle among his sons. Or perhaps the new ruler did not approve of fighting alongside Romans.

It is also possible that Aetius never intended to destroy Attila. The Huns had been allies for a long time, and they might still be useful in future disputes with the Visigoths. Wiping them out could weaken the Romans' already shaky grip on western Europe.

Attila watched in astonishment as the Romans withdrew. At first, he suspected a trap. Gradually, it became clear that he and his army were free to go. His weary soldiers picked themselves up and saddled their horses. They loaded the wounded in wagons and headed east for home. Nobody is sure how many dead were left behind. Between 15,000 and 30,000 men had probably been killed on the Catalaunian Fields.

Had Attila won his showdown with Aetius, the victory might have changed the course of history. The Huns could have extended their empire throughout western Europe. Christian churches might have

THE HUNS LOOK TO ATTILA for advice after their
defeat at the Catalaunian Fields. Attila was ready to set himself on
fire to avoid capture by the Romans.

disappeared in France, Italy, Spain, and Germany, replaced by the pagan rituals of the Huns.

Instead, the Huns retreated eastward to regroup. Attila's fortunetellers had been right about the Catalaunian Fields. A great commander—King Theodoric—did die on the battlefield. But the fortunetellers failed to predict other, more important consequences of the battle. They failed to see that the Catalaunian Fields would be the West Roman Empire's last great military victory. Rome's 800 years of dominance were finally coming to an end.

The fortunetellers also failed to see the most important outcome for Attila. The Hun king had reached the peak of his power. He was still a terror, still a mighty warlord with huge armies at his command. He would rise again, destroy cities, and crush enemies. But the defeat at the Catalaunian Fields spelled the beginning of the end for Attila's empire.

PART 4

Final Battles

CHAPTER 14

The Birds of Aquileia

Attila's superstition DOOMS A CITY.

ATTILA HAD BEEN TRAINED FROM BIRTH for battle. As he rose to power, fighting became a political necessity. To control his people, Attila needed loot to pay soldiers and conquests to supply him with new recruits. The king of the Huns needed war.

In the spring of 452, he created one. This time, he took a smaller army on the march—probably around 100,000 men. A small force would move quickly and be fairly easy to feed.

Attila also chose a new target. He saw that attacking Gaul again would reunite the Romans and Visigoths against him. But if Attila invaded the Roman heartland, the Visigoths would stand aside and let the Romans fight alone.

Attila set his sights on the city of Rome. Valentinian III, the West Roman emperor, lived in Ravenna, near Italy's eastern coast. But Rome was still the heart of the empire. Seizing the city—or even placing it in danger—would restore Attila's reputation as a warrior. As an added incentive, the 700-mile route to Rome presented plenty of wealthy cities for the Huns to plunder.

As Attila's men raced south and west into Italy, they reached the first prize of their campaign, a port city on the Adriatic Sea called Aquileia. Traders brought their goods to Aquileia from all over the empire. Jewish glassmakers in the city made some of the world's finest glassware. Aquileia boasted so much wealth and culture that people called it a "second Rome."

With riches to protect, the Aquileians made sure their city was well defended. High, thick walls and the waters of the Natisone River protected the city from attack.

Despite these obstacles, Attila decided he could not pass up such a rich prize. From June through July, his army tried to batter its way into Aquileia. The Huns swung huge battering rams against the gates. They used gigantic slings to hurl boulders at the walls. But the city's defenses held.

After weeks of frustration, Attila's men began to grumble. The soldiers wanted action, not a long siege. They also wanted loot, and time was running out. Armies seldom fought during the cold winter months.

One day in late summer, Attila was ready to call off the siege. But before he ordered his army to withdraw, he took one last walk around Aquileia's walls. He noticed some storks flying from the city with their young. Fortunetellers of the time closely followed the movement of birds. Roman armies even carried special chickens with them. If the chickens dropped some of their food while eating, soldiers believed that their next battle would go well.

Attila's fortunetellers saw the departing storks as a sign from heaven. According to Jordanes, Attila told his men, "Look at the birds, which foresee what is to come, leaving the doomed city, deserting endangered strongholds which are about to fall. Do not think this is without meaning. It is certain. They know what is going to happen. Fear of the future changes their habits."

ATTILA SPOTTED STORKS fleeing the city of Aquileia. He believed this was a sign that his siege would succeed.

BIRTH OF VENICE

ATTILA'S MARCH THROUGH ITALY IN 452 LEFT thousands of people homeless. Thousands of villagers hid their belongings and fled before the greed and bloodlust of the Huns.

According to tradition, refugees from Aquileia, Padua, and other nearby cities sought safety in a marsh known as Laguna Veneta. It was a soggy refuge crisscrossed by water channels, and Attila's horsemen found it impossible to give chase. Later invaders such as the Lombards forced still more refugees into the area. Over time, these refugees began building a great port on the Adriatic Sea. Today, it is known as the city of Venice.

ROMAN REFUGEES built Venice atop wooden posts hammered into the middle of a lagoon.

Attila's confidence breathed new life into the siege. His men redoubled their efforts with the battering rams and the slings. Before long, the Huns proved Attila's prediction right. Aquileia's walls began to crumble.

Attila's men poured into the city. Jordanes says that they "despoiled, smashed asunder, and devastated so savagely that they hardly left a trace of [the city] to be seen." Aquileia never regained its importance. Today, it is little more than a small town.

CHAPTER 15

Attila and the Pope

The Huns once again
STOP SHORT
AND GO HOME.

LATE IN THE SUMMER OF 452, ATTILA'S army continued its relentless march across northern Italy, carving a path from Aquileia to Milan.

Other cities tried to avoid Aquileia's fate. They threw open their gates to the Huns, hoping for mercy. Attila's men still burned and looted. But in most cases, the inhabitants had time to flee. Attila rolled brutally through the cities of Padua, Vicenza, Verona, Brescia, and Bergamo.

In Milan, Attila decided to set up camp for a while. For more than 100 years, until 402, the city had served as the capital of the West Roman Empire. Attila made his home in a palace once inhabited by generations of Roman emperors. One of the paintings in the palace caught his attention. It showed two Roman emperors looking down on a barbarian king, who groveled at their feet. Attila decided the painting needed revision, and he called in a local painter to do the job. In the new version, the two emperors could be seen piling gold at Attila's feet.

From Milan, Attila considered his next move. With the West Roman Empire no longer commanding the loyalty of its people, Aetius had failed to pull together an army large enough to oppose the Huns. The road to Rome lay open to Attila. Yet the Hun king decided not to take it.

Once again, fortunetellers played a role in the fate of the empire. They told Attila that taking Rome would mean disaster for the Huns. Attila, they said, would meet the same fate as the last barbarian king to sack Rome.

Alaric, the Visigoth king who overran the city in 410, died shortly after his great victory.

With this prediction in mind, Attila welcomed a group of envoys from the Roman emperor. Among them was Pope Leo I, head of the Catholic Church. Leo was a zealous leader, determined to advance the faith at all costs. He had burned anti-Christian books and ruthlessly persecuted anyone who did not hold Christian beliefs.

Many Christian accounts portray Leo as a hero in his meeting with Attila. They suggest that Leo's strength and piety tamed the wild Hun king. As one writer put it, "[Attila] was so flattered by the presence of the highest priest [Leo] that he ordered his men to stop the hostilities and, promising peace, returned beyond the Danube."

In reality, Leo probably handled Attila in a time-tested way: He bribed the Hun king to go home. Attila accepted the bribe because staying in Italy had proved to be harder than expected. Once again, disease had ripped

IN 452, POPE LEO convinced Attila to withdraw from Italy.
The pope probably offered the Hun king a significant bribe.

through the ranks of his army. Supplies were running short. And Attila's own fortunetellers had predicted doom if he pressed on to Rome.

Attila weighed his options, and in the autumn of 452, he ordered his men back to Pannonia.

As it would turn out, however, no retreat could keep bad fortune from closing in on the king of the Huns.

CHAPTER 16

A Wedding and a Funeral

Attila and his new wife have a DREADFUL WEDDING NIGHT.

IN THE SPRING OF 453, ATTILA HAD reached his mid-fifties. He was apparently in good health. And he still had dreams of conquest.

There were plenty of targets for Attila to choose from. The East Roman Emperor Marcian had already provoked Attila by refusing to send his annual payment of gold. Attila threatened to send an army charging down the Danube River to lay waste to Constantinople.

The West Romans still presented an easy target. Perhaps Attila meant to return to Italy and finish off Rome once and for all. Or perhaps he intended to play the schoolyard bully, extorting money from the West Romans by keeping them in fear.

Attila might have had other conquests in mind as well. Looking east, he would have seen the large and vulnerable Persian Empire in the Middle East. The Persians could have provided a rich new source of gold and slaves.

By yet another account, Attila was already punishing barbarian tribes that had sided with the Romans. He threatened the Visigoths in the west but then attacked the Alans to the east. "As he was shrewd and crafty, he threatened in one direction and moved his army in another," Jordanes wrote.

In the midst of his war plans, Attila married once again in the spring of 453. He had been sent a beautiful

German girl named Ildico as yet another bride. Lesser rulers often gave women to Hun kings as presents, much as they would give animal skins or jewelry.

Attila was not known for excessive revelry. But the Huns celebrated special occasions by giving many toasts. After each toast, the people present had to drink all the wine or beer in their glasses. Failure to do so was considered rude.

After feasting and drinking all night, Attila and Ildico went to bed. The next morning, the king of the Huns appeared to sleep late. That was no surprise. But hours passed and he still did not appear. Aides knocked anxiously at the door but heard only sobbing on the other side.

Frightened, they finally kicked in the door. What they found shocked everyone. Attila, king of the Huns, lay on his bed in a puddle of blood. At first, it looked like he had been murdered. But there were no signs of violence. It soon became clear that Attila had coughed up blood in his sleep. The hemorrhage may have been caused by a burst artery or vein. Perhaps an ulcer was to blame.

Whatever the cause, Attila choked on his own blood and died. Ildico went to bed with the king of the Huns and woke up beside a corpse. Apparently, she was too terrified to call for help.

Historians have wondered whether Ildico did in fact murder Attila. But Attila's aides did not think so. A speech given at Attila's funeral promised no punishment or vengeance. "He fell neither by an enemy's blow nor by treachery," the speaker said, "but safe among his own people, happy, rejoicing, without any pain."

Attila's funeral followed nomadic traditions. His body lay under a silk tent on the windy plain. Hun warriors galloped around the tent singing songs of praise. Each soldier's face was stained with his own blood. The men had sliced their cheeks and cut off hunks of hair to show their grief.

Attila was buried amid great secrecy. A small army of slaves dug his tomb in the dead of night. Attila's men

ILDICO WEEPS at the feet of her dead husband, Attila. Without
their ruthless king to hold them together, the Huns would be
pushed back into Asia, where they would fade from history.

feared that grave robbers might try to dig up the gold and gems buried with their king. So they surprised the burial party and slaughtered the slaves. The location of Attila's grave would remain a secret forever.

With that final massacre, Attila the Hun passed into legend.

Wicked?

Attila's death was surprising yet somewhat fitting. A conqueror who glutted himself with the blood of others died choking on his own.

Fortunetellers once claimed that the Huns would decline after Attila, only to be revived by his youngest son. History proved them right on the first prediction and wrong on the second.

After Attila's death, his sons squabbled over control of the empire. The civil war crippled the Huns, who were then defeated by the East Roman Empire and rival barbarian tribes. The East Romans stuck the head of one of Attila's sons on a pole and carried it proudly through the streets of Constantinople. By 469, the Huns had been chased to southern Russia, where they merged with other tribes. The Hun threat to Europe had died with Attila.

The West Roman Empire faded almost as quickly. With Attila dead, Valentinian saw no reason to keep Aetius around. In 454, the emperor personally stabbed

Aetius to death. Aetius's bodyguards got revenge, stabbing Valentinian to death the following year. Nine emperors ruled over the next 21 years. Of them, two were deposed and six died violently. The last emperor, Augustulus, was overthrown by a barbarian in 476. The West Roman Empire had been swept away.

Corruption and intrigue also plagued the East Romans. Yet their empire lasted another 1,000 years, becoming known as the Byzantine Empire. As Attila had learned, Constantinople was nearly impossible to attack. No army was able to breach the city's walls until after the invention of cannons.

Nearly 1,500 years after Attila's death, the question remains: Was he truly as wicked as his reputation? It's hard to tell from ancient accounts of the Hun king's life. Most of them were written by Attila's enemies, either Romans or Visigoths. They naturally paint him in a negative light. Modern Hungarians, on the other hand, consider Attila a national hero. Some Hungarians even name their sons after him.

Overall, though, Attila's legacy remains a dark one. His most important achievement was to help topple the West Roman Empire. Weak as it was, the empire had spread culture and order throughout Europe. When it disappeared, schools closed, roads fell into disrepair, trade declined, and scientific study stalled. Life in Europe became more primitive for the next five centuries.

Attila did not usher in this Dark Age alone. He got the blame because he was a pagan leader in an increasingly Christian world. Many paintings done after Attila's death showed the Hun leader with the horns and pointed ears of a devil.

While Attila's crimes have been exaggerated, the terror he inspired has not. "Attila ground almost the whole of Europe into dust," one contemporary wrote. Today, most people know little about Attila's deeds. Yet his name remains a household word that signifies ruthlessness and destruction. Attila is a bogeyman that people can't seem to forget.

Timeline of Terror

376

376: Barbarian tribes, fleeing the Huns, cross the Danube River into Roman territory.

c. 400: Attila is born.

410: Hun King Uldin launches a failed invasion of the East Roman Empire.

410: The Visigoths sack Rome. They later set up their own kingdom in southeastern Gaul.

435: Hun King Ruga dies. Attila and Bleda become co-kings. They kill many rivals to consolidate their power.

439: Vandals capture North Africa, robbing the West Romans of their richest province.

444: Attila murders Bleda and becomes sole king of the Huns.

447: An earthquake destroys many of Constantinople's walls. Attila attacks but fails to seize the city.

449: Priscus visits Attila's capital. The East Romans make an unsuccessful attempt to assassinate Attila.

451: Attila invades Gaul. He is turned back at the Battle of Catalaunian Fields.

452: Attila invades Italy, destroys the city of Aquileia, and sacks several other cities before turning back.

453: Attila dies. Within 16 years, the Hun Empire dissolves.

453

GLOSSARY

ambassador (am-BASS-uh-dur) *noun* a person sent by a government to represent that government in another country

assassinate (uh-SASS-uh-nate) *verb* to murder someone who is well-known or important

avenge (uh-VENJ) *verb* to inflict harm in return for a wrong done to oneself or another

barbarians (bar-BAIR-ee-uhnz) *noun* people from various tribes that invaded the Roman Empire during the third to fifth centuries A.D.

battering ram (BAT-ur-ing RAM) *noun* a large wooden weapon that was used to break down city walls

catapult (KAT-uh-puhlt) *noun* a weapon, similar to a large slingshot, used for firing rocks over walls

cavalry (KAV-uhl-ree) *noun* soldiers who ride on horseback

consolidate (kuhn-SOL-uh-date) *verb* to bring several different parts together into one

corruption (kuh-RUHP-shun) *noun* the use of public office for private gain

coup (KOO) *noun* a sudden, violent, and illegal seizure of power

demoralize (di-MOR-uh-lize) *verb* to cause to lose confidence or hope

deploy (di-PLOY) *verb* to move troops into position for military action

depose (di-POZE) *verb* to remove from office suddenly and forcefully

devastate (DEV-uh-stayt) *verb* to cause great distress, damage, or destruction

devout (di-VOUT) *adjective* deeply religious

divine (duh-VINE) *adjective* to do with or from God

empire (EM-pire) *noun* a group of countries or regions that have the same ruler

envoy (ON-voy) *noun* a person appointed to represent one government in its dealings with another

formidable (FOR-mih-duh-buhl) *adjective* inspiring fear or respect through being impressively powerful

impale (im-PAIL) *verb* to torture or kill by piercing with a sharp stake

legion (LEE-juhn) *noun* in the late Roman Empire, a military unit made up of about 1,000 men, each armed with a long, thrusting spear

monastery (MON-uh-ster-ee) *noun* a group of buildings where monks live and work

monk (MUHNGK) *noun* a man who lives in a religious community and has promised to devote his life to his God

negotiate (ni-GOH-shee-ate) *verb* to discuss something in order to come to an agreement

nomad (NOH-mad) *noun* a person who wanders from place to place

pagan (PAY-guhn) *noun* a person who is not a member of the Christian, Jewish, or Muslim religions; a pagan may worship many gods or have no religion at all

pillage (PILL-ij) *verb* to rob using violence, especially in wartime

proposition (prop-uh-ZI-shuhn) *noun* an offer or suggestion

province (PROV-uhnss) *noun* a district or region of a country or empire

refugee (ref-yuh-JEE) *noun* a person who is forced to leave his or her home because of war, persecution, or a natural disaster

reprieve (ri-PREEV) *noun* a postponement of a punishment

savagery (SAV-ij-ree) *noun* behavior that is fierce, violent, and uncontrolled

scourge (SKURJ) *noun* a cause of great harm and suffering

siege (SEEJ) *noun* the surrounding of a place, such as a castle or city, to cut off supplies and then wait for those inside to surrender

successor (suhk-SESS-ur) *noun* one who follows another in a position of leadership

FIND OUT MORE

Here are some books and Web sites with more information about Attila the Hun and his times.

BOOKS

Harvey, Bonnie C. **Attila the Hun (Ancient World Leaders)**. Philadelphia: Chelsea House, 2003. (100 pages) *Describes the life of Attila and his attempt to conquer the Roman Empire.*

Ingram, Scott. **Attila the Hun**. San Diego: Blackbirch Press, 2003. (112 pages) *Discusses the Roman Empire, its collapse at the hands of barbarian hordes led by Attila the Hun, and Attila's legacy.*

Nardo, Don. **The Fall of the Roman Empire**. Farmington Hills, Mich: Lucent Books, 2004. (112 pages) *Explores the reasons for the decline and fall of the Roman Empire, including the invasions of the barbarians, the weakening of the Roman legions, and the growth of Christianity.*

Oliver, Marilyn Tower. **Attila the Hun (Heroes and Villains)**. Farmington Hills, Mich: Lucent Books, 2006. (112 pages) *A well-written, balanced look at the life of Attila. Includes quotes from primary-source documents.*

Williams, Stephen, and Gerard Friell. **The Rome that Did Not Fall: The Survival of the East in the Fifth Century**. New York: Routledge, 1999. (304 pages) *Examines how, in the fifth century, the West Roman Empire collapsed while the East Roman Empire survived and consolidated its power in the face of invading barbarians.*

WEB SITES

http://encarta.msn.com/encyclopedia_761552863/attila.html
MSN Encarta's online encyclopedia article about Attila the Hun.

http://www.bbc.co.uk/history/ancient/romans
This BBC site, Ancient History: Romans, features articles on Roman emperors and the fall of Rome, as well as a link to "Rome's Greatest Enemies Gallery," which profiles six of Rome's greatest adversaries, including Attila the Hun.

http://www.fordham.edu/halsall/source/attila1.html
This is a translation of Priscus's eyewitness description of Attila and his court in 449.

For Grolier subscribers:
http://go.grolier.com/ searches: Attila; Aetius, Flavius; Theodoric I; Istanbul

INDEX

AUTHOR'S NOTE AND BIBLIOGRAPHY

Attila the Hun challenges any historian. Only one eyewitness, the East Roman Priscus, left a record of what Attila was like personally. The rest of our information about him comes from secondhand sources, people who never met the man himself. The Huns left no written records at all.

Yet we know enough to grasp the breadth of Attila's ambitions and the depth of his ruthlessness. Some of these books, like Gibbon's *Decline and Fall of the Roman Empire*, are very old. But they are still worth reading for anyone who wants to understand Attila and his fascinating, chaotic world.

The following books have been most useful in telling Attila's story:

Browersock, G.W. et al., editors. Late Antiquity: A Guide to the Postclassical World. Cambridge, MA: Harvard University Press, 1999.

Bury, J.B. The Invasion of Europe by the Barbarians. New York: Norton & Co., 1967.

Gibbon, Edward. The Decline and Fall of the Roman Empire, Vol. III. New York: Alfred A. Knopf, 1993.

Gordon, C.D. The Age of Attila: Fifth-Century Byzantium and the Barbarians. Ann Arbor, MI: University of Michigan Press, 1960.

Heather, Peter. The Fall of the Roman Empire: A New History of Rome and the Barbarians. New York: Oxford University Press, 2006.

Howarth, Patrick. Attila, King of the Huns: Man and Myth. New York: Barnes & Noble Books, 1995.

Maenchen-Helfen, Otto J. The World of the Huns: Studies in Their History and Culture. Berkeley, CA: University of California Press, 1973.

Man, John. Attila: The Barbarian King Who Challenged Rome. New York: St. Martin's Press, 2005.

Oost, Stewart Irvin. Galla Placidia Augusta: A Biographical Essay. Chicago: University of Chicago Press, 1968.

Ward-Perkins, Bryan. The Fall of Rome and the End of Civilization. New York: Oxford University Press, 2005.

—Sean Stewart Price